D0583679

Saron,
Enjoy your Birthday!
look Happy

Love
Denise :!

THE
BOOK OF KELLS

THE
BOOK OF KELLS

TEXT COMPILED BY
BEN MACKWORTH-PRAED

HarperSanFrancisco
A Division of HarperCollins*Publishers*

Frontispiece:
The Eagle, symbol of St John, from the
Book of Kells.

FIRST HARPERCOLLINS EDITION PUBLISHED IN 1995

Printed in Singapore.

ISBN 0-06-251131-9

95 96 97 98 99 SGP 10 9 8 7 6 5 4 3 2 1

INTRODUCTION

The *Book of Kells* is the richest, most copiously illuminated, manuscript version of the four Gospels in the Celto-Saxon style that still survives. But considering its fame, it is surprising that relatively little is known about it.

It consists of 339 vellum leaves, or folios, each one disastrously cropped by a nineteenth-century bookbinder, and covered with beautifully formed, black-ink script, the initial letters picked out in brightly coloured paints and ornamented with fantastic abstract animal and human forms.

We know that it once had more pages, for when Archbishop Ussher bought the book in 1621, he wrote in it that there were 344 folios. We think, judging by the parts missing from the Gospels of St Luke and St John that there may have been as many as 368 folios.

In fact it is surprising that so much of the book does survive! The Abbey of Kells, from where it is first known, was plundered at least seven times before 1006, when the book was stolen and buried for three months. When it was recovered its jewel-encrusted, golden cover had gone forever.

On the dissolution of the Abbey, the book probably passed to the family of the last abbot, and may have had several owners before being collected by Archbishop Ussher. When he died his daughter tried to sell it in Europe; Oliver Cromwell blocked this, and the book was sold to the army in Ireland instead. For five years it lay in an open room in Dublin Castle until 1661 when Charles II presented it to Ussher's *alma mater*, Trinity College, Dublin where it remains.

That much we know. We do not know when or where the book was written or even who wrote it, although, according to legend, St Columba was the creator of this, perhaps the most beautiful of books.

Before the invention of printing, the Gospels and other holy writings were copied out by hand. Conscious of the intrinsic value of a book as the sum of so many laborious hours, and the spiritual value of these works, the scribes took to ornamenting their manuscripts richly.

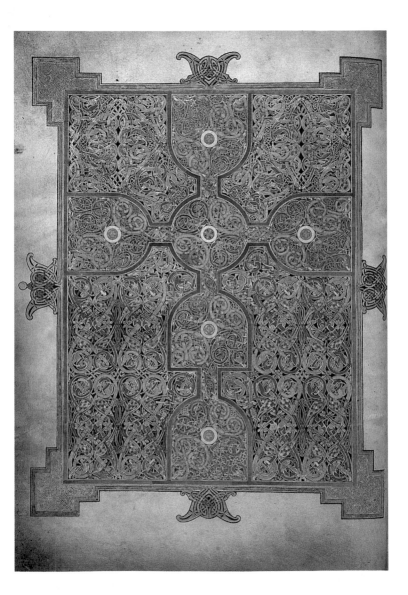

Every region where Christianity flourished produced Gospels in its own particular style. But few decorated them with such magnificence as the monks of northern Britain and Ireland where the so-called 'Insular' style evolved and flourished.

While Byzantine, Italian and Saxon art all influenced the Insular style, its mainspring was the skill in decorating metalwork and leather which the Celts brought with them when they arrived in Ireland from mainland Europe and Britain in pre-Christian times.

There were already isolated Christian communities in Ireland before St Patrick's arrival there in 432. Pre-Christian culture that did not clash with Christianity was pressed into Christian service, and so the Celtic tradition of ornament was given a new outlet in the decoration of religious books that the new Church required.

In 563, St Columba, said to be the founder of the Abbey at Kells as well as the creator of its famous book, left Ireland for Iona in Scotland where he established a monastery

that flourished for nearly 250 years.

By then in England, successive Saxon invasions had effectively wiped out Christianity, and it was not until 597, when St Augustine from Rome arrived in Kent that the religion was re-established in England.

Christianity was taken to northern England when a Christian, Kentish princess married Edwin of Northumbria. The couple's heirs were sent to Iona to be educated and, later, invited St Aidan to come from there to found a monastery at Lindisfarne.

Aidan and his monks brought with them the Celtic traditions of illuminating manuscripts, examples of which can be seen in the *Cathach of St Columba*, the *Codex Ussherianus Primus* and the *Book of Durrow*. At Lindisfarne, mingling these Celtic traditions with native Saxon art and the influences of Rome and Byzantine, the monks created the marvellous *Durham Gospels* and *Book of Lindisfarne*.

Aidan's monks also brought the traditions of their Celtic church, including gospels that pre-dated St Jerome's Vulgate, his fourth-century translation from original texts. Any attempt to date the *Book of Kells* must account

Opposite
A portrait of St Matthew from the *Book of Lindisfarne* showing the Mediterranean influence on manuscript art.

for the extent to which its text varies from both the Vulgate and other Celtic gospels.

Another clue to the *Book of Kells'* date lies in the fact that it contains a greater variety of elements than any of the other Insular manuscripts mentioned above. All the main strands of Celtic illumination can be found in its pages. In abstract patterns alone, there are diverging and interlocking spirals that spring from indigenous Celtic decorations, interlocking ribbons perhaps derived from everyday, three-dimensional examples such as torques of braided wires, and frets, probably Mediterranean in origin, but with the Celtic addition of 45-degree angles.

Animal heads, legs and tails, added to the extremities of letters, appeared early in Insular manuscripts, but leaf patterns are seldom seen before about 800. They probably grew more from the habit of ornamenting animal tails with 'feathers' that gradually took on the appearance of leaves, rather than from conscious imitation of continental examples. Both are present in the *Book of Kells* along with the addition of animal heads to interlace, a feature which first appears in the *Book of Lindisfarne* and which, in the *Book of Kells*, is extended to human form also.

All this evidence suggests that the *Book of Kells* should be considered the culmination of the Insular tradition. Linking its writing to Iona in the years immediately before repeated Viking attacks drove the monks to Kells in 807, gives rational explanations for its attribution to St Columba, the incompleteness of some of its illustrations and its present name.

Perhaps the most striking aspect of the *Book of Kells* is the immense disparity between the consummate draughtsmanship of the decorations and the crudity of the portraits of human figures. These figures may be deliberately naive, the subjects too holy to be drawn representationally. In the eleventh century at Mount Athos in Greece, and the thirteenth century at Ballymote in Ireland, guides were established setting out how each saint should be drawn. Before that, what could have been more logical than to copy faithfully an earlier, if inferior model, even if the result became stylized, even heraldic?

Similarly, in the pages that introduce each Gospel, where the decoration so puzzlingly swamps the opening words as to make them unintelligible to anyone who does not already know what they should be, the suggestion has been made that this, too, is deliberate, a symbolic portal through which only initiates may pass to the knowledge so magnificently presented within.

— THE —
PLATES

PLATE I

A PAGE OF THE EUSEBIAN CANONS

Fol. 5R

The Eusebian Canons were devised by Eusebius, a fourth-century Bishop of Caesarea to demonstrate the relationship between the Gospels by citing parallel passages in each. The numbers in the tables refer to a system of division of each Gospel also devised by Eusebius before the adoption of the modern system of chapters and verses. The rather dry columns of figures were often livened in early manuscripts by being placed between the columns of an arcade in which adjacent columns were joined by arches containing the names or symbols of the Evangelists, the whole being surmounted by a larger arch spanning all the columns. The artist of the *Book of Kells* has moved the four Symbols (the Man for St Matthew, the Lion for St Mark, the Ox for St Luke and the Eagle for St John) up into the spandrels and tympanum of the main arch, and introduced the wealth of all of the types of ornamentation for which the manuscript is renowned into both arches and columns.

PLATE II

THE VIRGIN AND CHILD

Fol. 7V

Professor Westwood in his *Palaeographia Sacra Pictoria* of 1843 draws attention to the contrast between the draughtsmanship of the central figures, which he describes as 'utterly puerile' and 'the ingenuity displayed in the sides and upper part of the drawing', possibly arising from a belief that sacred figures should be drawn in an 'heraldic' rather than 'representational' style. Neither he, nor Sir Edward Sullivan after him, have any explanation for the six averted heads in the small panel breaking the right-hand margin, but Sullivan has remarked that the Virgin has two right feet and her offspring two left ones.

PLATE III

PORTION OF THE 'ARGUMENTA' TO THE GOSPEL OF ST JOHN AND 'BREVES CAUSAE' OF ST LUKE

Fol. 19V

Chapter headings (*breves causae*) and summaries (*argumenta*) were frequently added to early Gospel manuscripts, and indeed some of those in the *Book of Kells* itself are written in a different hand and in varying colours of ink. This particular page however, is in the same hand and style as the main portions of the Gospels, and exhibits a number of characteristics shared with other contemporary Irish manuscripts, in particular the symbol, 'C'. Known as the 'head under the wing' or the 'turn in the path' it appears three times in various guises, and indicates that all after it on that line properly belongs to the end of the following line: it has been written above that line to fill a space left after a full-stop in the first line.

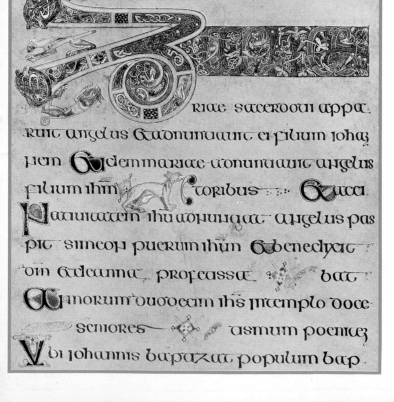

exponitur uesciendi desiderio collocato &

quaerentibus fructus laboris & do magiste

rii doctrina seruituri

riae sacerdoti appa

ruit angelus & adnuntiauit ei filium Johan

nem & idem mariae adnuntiauit angelus

filium ihm toribus & uca

Natiuitatem ihu adiungat angelus pas

pit siincon puerum ihm & benedicat

dni & deanna profeassa bat

Annorum duodecim ihs in templo doce

seniores usmum poenitæ

Vbi Johannis baptizat populum bap

PLATE IV

THE EVANGELICAL SYMBOLS

Fol. 27V

This plate portrays the symbols of the four Evangelists, adopted at an early stage of Christianity from the four beasts of Ezekiel and the Book of Revelation, later re-organized by St Jerome. The Man is for St Matthew, in recognition of his emphasis on the human side of the Saviour. The Lion represents St Mark, who stressed Christ's power and royalty. The Ox or calf stands for St Luke, a sacrificial victim in token of his emphasis on Christ's priesthood. The Eagle is for St John, the Evangelist who soars to Heaven, as St Augustine puts it, and gazes on the light of immutable truth with keen and undazzled eyes. Symbols, often pagan in origin, played an important role in the life of the early and medieval Church. Among them are the fish, an acronym, in Greek, for Jesus Christ, the peacock for immortality (see Plate VII) and the stag for the soul thirsting for redemption.

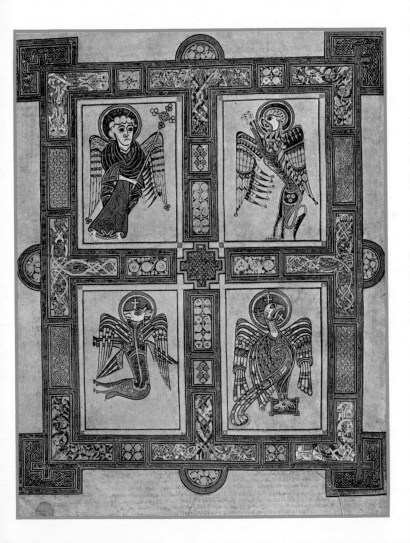

PLATE V

PORTRAIT OF ST MATTHEW

Fol. 28V

Each of the four Gospels in the *Book of Kells* appears originally to have been prefaced by a portrait of its author. Today, only those of Sts Matthew and John are now to be found in their correct positions (Fol. 28V and Fol. 29IV respectively). They appear immediately before the opening words of their respective Gospels (Fols 29R and 292R), while a portrait showing close similarities in style and border to these may be found in Fol. 32V (see Plate VII). St Matthew is depicted here standing barefoot in front of (or just possibly sitting on) a throne. The back of it is decorated with lions' heads, the symbol of St Mark, and the arms are embellished with the calf and eagle of Sts Luke and John. Matthew's right hand is buried in the folds of his robe, while his exposed left hand holds a copy of his Gospel. The image is surrounded by a border heavily ornamented with spiral motifs.

PLATE VI

THE OPENING WORDS OF
ST MATTHEW'S GOSPEL

Fol. 29R

The first words of St Matthew's Gospel are *'Liber generationis'*. The page is one of the most highly decorated in the *Book of Kells* and strongly resembles the corresponding, but far less ornate page in the *Book of Lindisfarne* (which almost certainly dates from the years immediately preceding 698). The figure in the lower left-hand corner holding a book, is thought to be another portrait of St Matthew, who may also be the figure at the head of the page. The much more crudely drawn lower figure may be a later addition by another hand, and there are several places left unfinished in the original design. The small face to the left of the upright portion of the 'L' lacks features and the portion of border above it and to its right is undecorated. Even more noticeable is the curiously intertwined 'ER' in the centre of the antique 'B' of 'LIBER' where most of the black border has been omitted from the 'E'.

Liber generationis
Ihu
Xpi filii

29

PLATE VII

PORTRAIT OF ST MARK OR ST LUKE

Fol. 32V

This so-called 'Doubtful Portrait' comes immediately after the Genealogy of Christ and has been taken as a portrait of Christ attended by Angels. However, it is more likely to be the portrait of either St Mark or St Luke, both of which are missing from the front of their Gospels. The format of the picture, and the details of the border, are remarkably similar to those of the portrait of St Matthew in Plate V, though less so to those of St John in Plate XXI. Also, in view of what has been noted in regard to the stylized nature of the representations of holy figures in manuscripts of this date, the face in this portrait bears little resemblance to the portraits of Christ in Plates XI and XX, and a great deal more to a portrait clearly identified as St Luke in the earlier Gospels of St Chad. The lack of any evangelical symbol could be explained by the two blank spandrels, though the presence of the twin peacocks, symbolic of immortality, in the tympanum remains disturbing.

PLATE VIII

THE EIGHT-CIRCLED CROSS

Fol. 33R

This is the only example of a 'carpet-cross' in the *Book of Kells*, though several similarly decorated simple crosses occur in the *Book of Lindisfarne*. Some authors believe that each of the Gospels in the *Book of Kells* was originally heralded by such a page. It is also unusual in being a 'Patriarchal' or double-armed cross, an echo perhaps of the carpet-cross which introduces the *Book of Durrow*. That cross is supposed in turn to resemble the carpet-page at the beginning of the Persian *Diatessaron Codex* in Florence. None of its predecessors, however, with the possible exception of the *Book of Lindisfarne*, can rival the Kells' cross for its intricacy and delicate execution. The medallions forming the extremities and junctions of the cross are reminiscent of Celtic metalwork at its finest, as may be seen in the Tara Brooch in the National Museum of Ireland in Dublin, or the Sutton Hoo Treasure in the British Museum.

PLATE IX

THE INCARNATION INITIAL

Fol. 34R

This is also known as the 'Monogram Page'. It is undoubtedly the most celebrated page of the entire book, and perhaps, as has been suggested, the most elaborate specimen of calligraphy ever executed. It consists of the phrase XRI B GENERATIO ('Christi autem generatio'), the opening words of St Matthew i. 18, 'Now the birth of Jesus Christ (was on this wise:)', and contains examples of almost all the varieties of design to be found in Celtic art. Among its glories are two moths and three angels in the left-hand quadrant of the 'X', and rats eating the showbread, while being watched by two cats, which some have seen as an allusion to unworthy communicants.

PLATE X

A PAGE FROM ST MATTHEW'S GOSPEL

Fol. 104R

This page, once mistakenly described as being from St Mark's Gospel, is in fact St Matthew xxiv. 19–24, so the contention that this page illustrates some of the textual differences between the Vulgate and the *Book of Kells* falls to the ground. The two texts do differ on occasions; this, however is not one of them. The page has some fine examples of both elongated animals and humans forming some of the capital letters and a seemingly irrelevant illustration filling space in a line. The two good examples of the abbreviation sign, five and four lines from the end of the page over the words 'Christus' and 'Christi' respectively, may, it has been claimed, also be seen in the ornamental line over the 'X' in the previous plate.

e autem praegnantibus et
nutrientibus in illis diebus :⁑

Orate autem ut non fiat fuga
uestra hieme uel sabbato

Erit enim tunc tribulatio magna
qualis non fuit ab initio mun
di usque modo neque fiet :⁑

Et nisi breuiata fuissent dies
illi non fiera salua om
nis caro sed propter electos bre
uiabuntur dies illi :⁑

Tunc si quis uobis dixerit ecce
hic xpc aut illic nolite credere

Surgent enim pseudo xpi et
pseudo prophetae et dabunt
signa magna et prodigia ita in erro
rem inducantur si fieri potest etiam

PLATE XI

THE ARREST OF CHRIST

Fol. 114R

This is one of the very few instances in the *Book of Kells* of the representation of an incident, rather than a formal portrait or abstract decoration. The figures are again stylized, almost naive, but the device of making Christ so much larger than His assailants thrusts Him forward out of the picture. This, together with His enormous, staring eyes, creates a moment of frozen horror that contrasts most effectively with both the formal setting of the comparatively austerely decorated arch, and the tranquillity of the words inscribed in the tympanum: 'And when they had sung an hymn, they went out into the mount of Olives' (Matthew xxvi. 30). The strict symmetry of the composition, broken only by the differing handholds of the sinister black-bearded, red-mustachioed guards, and the sprawling trefoil plants, no doubt a reference to the Garden of Gethsemane, above their heads, does nothing to counteract this feeling of menace.

PLATE XII

THE CRUCIFIXION PAGE

Fol. 124R

This passage 'TUNC CRUCIFIXERANT XRI CUM EO DUOS LATRONES' is from Matthew xxvii. 38, 'Then were there two thieves crucified with him.' The XRI appears to be redundant. The Vulgate Latin reads, '*Tunc crucifixi sunt*' which is in agreement with the English, this being one of the passages in which it does differ from the *Book of Kells*. It has been suggested that it may be a survival of a medieval notemark, known as a 'Chrismon' and composed of a monogram of '*Christi*'. This device was frequently used to draw attention to important passages, but has somehow in this case become incorporated in the text. J. O. Westwood draws particular attention to the initial 'T', 'formed of a most singular quadruped, vomiting forth horned serpents'. No less curious are the three panels of heads in profile, perhaps onlookers, reminiscent of the mysterious six heads in the border of the 'Virgin and Child' in Plate II.

PLATE XIII

THE EVANGELICAL SYMBOLS

Fol. 129V

This page of Evangelical Symbols introduces St Mark's Gospel. It is considerably more ornate than that which began St Matthew's, though similar in form. It retains the format of a St George's cross, here embellished with circles round the symbols themselves, whereas those introducing St Luke's and St John's Gospels are arranged in the form of a saltire. The symbols also appear more than once on the page, both in their own and other Evangelists' quadrants. In each case though, the primary symbol is clearly distinguished by the circle mentioned above and by a pair of floral sceptres. The cross and outer frame are more finely ornamented than in the previous example (see Plate IV). This gives this page a feeling of lightness not apparent in the other. However, the overall effect is inexplicably marred by a disparity in length between the two horizontal arms of the lower 'T' at the bottom of the page, and the misplacement of the external embellishment. According to Sullivan, this is the only instance of such an error in the whole manuscript.

PLATE XIV

THE OPENING WORDS OF ST MARK'S GOSPEL

Fol. 130R

The first few words of this Gospel, 'INITIUM EVANGELII IHU XRI', 'The beginning of the gospel of Jesus Christ', again occupy a whole page of the manuscript. The first 'I' is more than a foot high in the original, and the whole is ornamented with extraordinary magnificence. Singled out for special attention has been the beautiful effect produced by the interlaced snakes at the four corners of the letter 'N'. The human figure at the top is held in the clasp of a dragon. Sullivan, maintains that the human is St Mark, and the 'dragon' his Lion which he is helping to devour the red serpent. He compares it to the 'quadruped' of Plate XII, which is similarly engaged, though in that case without evangelical assistance.

PLATE XV

A PAGE FROM ST MARK'S GOSPEL

Fol. 183V

This page, from Mark xv. 25–31, descri-bes the crucifixion. Written normally at seventeen lines to the page of text, apart from some short passages clearly in another hand and often in differing coloured inks, it is so uniform as to appear almost certainly the work of one man. Moreover, the illuminated initials are so intimately worked into the lines of the text that not only were they laid out and painted by the same man, but also they must have been executed simultaneously with the text. The initials throughout the book fall into two main types: a black outline with coloured or decorated interstices, or a fully coloured monogram where the original letter is incorporated into, and indeed often as here almost submerged by, the efflorescence of the design.

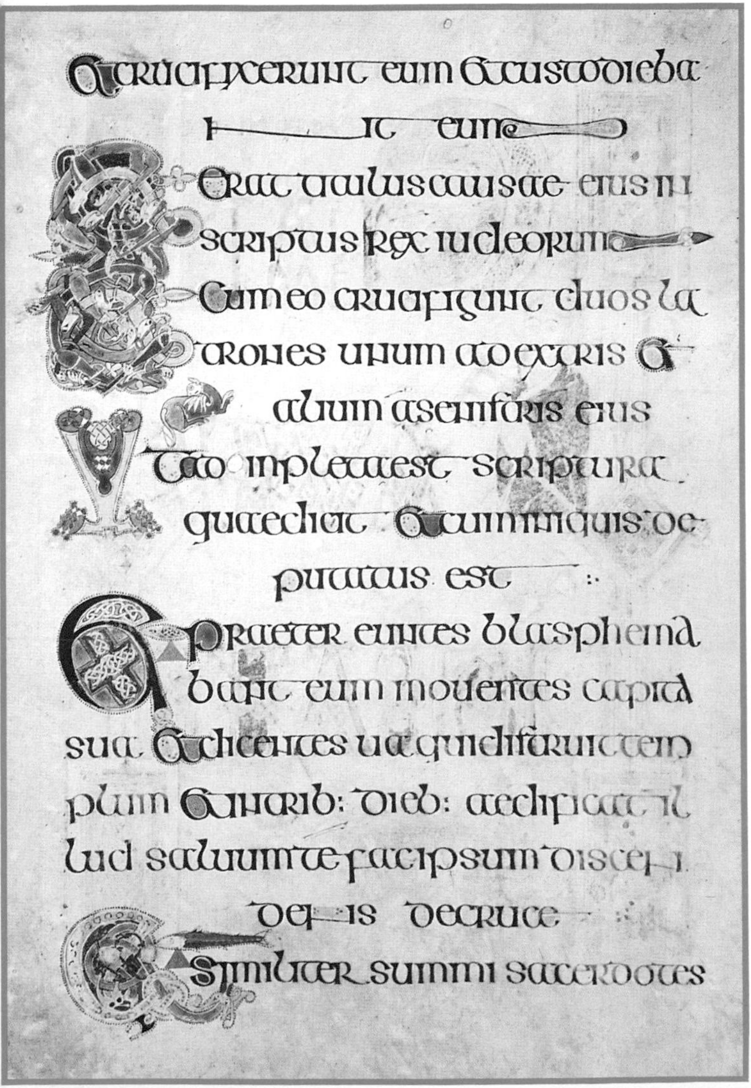

Et CRUCIFIXERUNT eum & custodieba

t eum

ERAT titulus causae eius in

scriptus REX IUdeORUM

Cum eo CRUCIFIGUNT duos la

trones unum ad extris &

alium a sinistris eius

Et adimpleta est scriptura

quae dicit et cum iniquis de

putatus est

Praetereuntes blasphema

bant eum mouentes capita

sua & dicentes uah qui destruit tem

plum & in trib: dieb: aedificat il

lud saluum te faci ipsum disce[n]

det is decruce

SImiliter summi sacerdotes

PLATE XVI

THE OPENING WORD OF ST LUKE'S GOSPEL

Fol. 188R

The whole of this page is taken up by the single word 'Quoniam', 'Forasmuch' in the Authorised Version. Some commentators, including Westwood, hold it to be the shortened form, 'Qniam'. Others maintain that the 'U' and 'O' are both to be seen in the diamond in the centre of the 'Q', the former in the form of a 'V' and the latter as a Greek omega. Sir Edward Sullivan wrote that, 'The crowd of figures intermixed with the letters NIAM may possibly have been suggested by the words which follow – '*multi conati sunt ordinare narrationem.*' But it is not at all obvious that these people are actively engaged in evangelism. They may equally well be there for purely decorative reasons, to allow the 'Q' to stand out from the rest of the composition. Note, too, the rear legs appearing below the foot of the border of the monster whose head appears above it. The loss of both top and left hand margins results from appalling book-binding.

PLATE XVII

THE GENEALOGY OF CHRIST
(Page 1)

Fol. 200R

It is curious that St Luke repeated a genealogy of Christ which has to be spurious if the central tenet of Christianity is to be believed. But thankfully he did for the pages beginning the genealogies are some of the most pleasingly harmonious in the entire manuscript. They combine the repetition of a single letter, 'Q', more than 70 times, with an ingenuity that allows no two letters to be the same. Yet at the same time each page is presented as a complete and co-ordinated whole. This page (Luke iii. 22–26) reads:

FACTA EST TU ES FILIUS MEUS DILECTUS EN TE BENE CONPLACUIT MIHI. ET IPSE IHS ERAT INCIPIENS QUASI ANNORUM TRIGIN-TA UT PUTABATUR FILIUS IOSEPH.

'... Thou art my beloved Son; in thee I am well pleased. And Jesus himself began to be about thirty years of age, being (as was supposed) the son of Joseph.'

The manuscript then goes on to list Joseph's ancestry back to Adam, covering five pages in all.

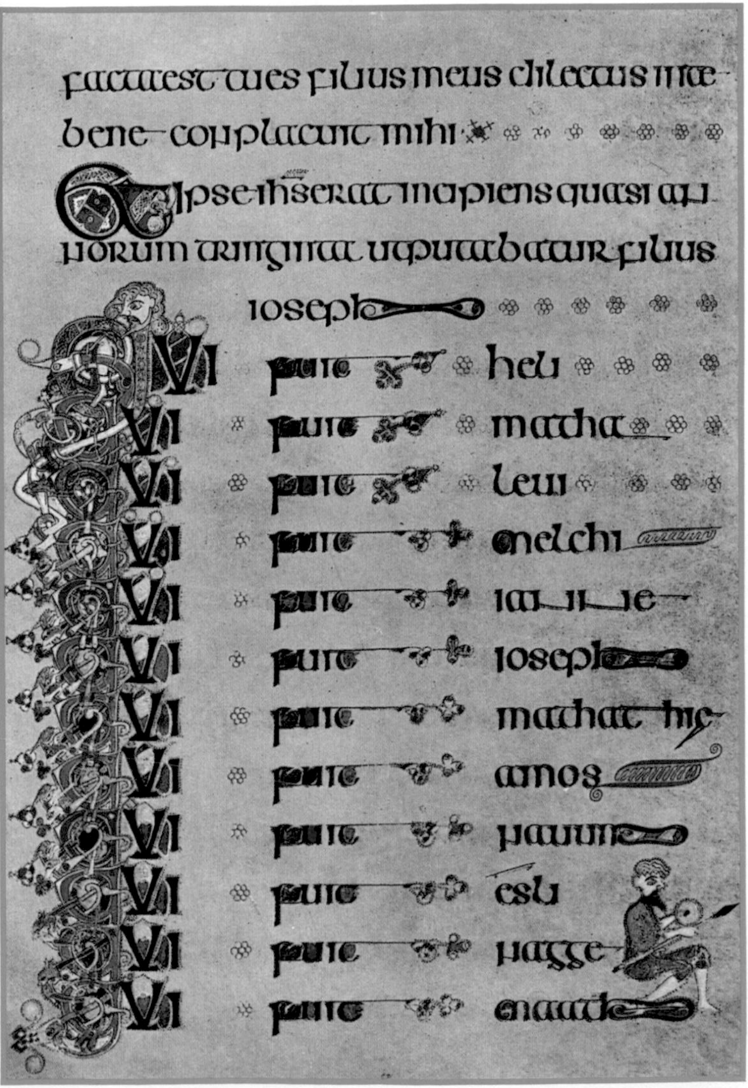

facta est tu es filius meus dilectus in te

bene complacuit mihi ❋ ❀ ❀ ❀ ❀ ❀ ❀

Ipse ihserat incipiens quasi an

horum triginta ut putabatur filius

ioseph ❀ ❀ ❀ ❀ ❀ ❀

V̄i   fuit   heli ❀ ❀

V̄i   fuit   matha ❀

V̄i   fuit   levi ❀

V̄i   fuit   melchi

V̄i   fuit   iannae

V̄i   fuit   ioseph

V̄i   fuit   mathat hic

V̄i   fuit   amos

V̄i   fuit   nauum

V̄i   fuit   esli

V̄i   fuit   nagge

V̄i   fuit   enaath

PLATE XVIII

THE GENEALOGY OF CHRIST
(Page 2)

Fol. 200V

O n the first page of the Genealogy, the animal-headed tails to the 'Q's strove furiously first against the elongated human at the head of the page and lower down against the curious bird-like creatures rising from the centre of succeeding letters. On this page the bird figures have turned their backs on the tails. This has left the dog-heads apparently puzzled by the disappear-ance of their opponents, except in the few cases where the birds' necks have extended themselves sufficiently to allow them to fight over their shoulders. There is an error in the first two lines. They should read, 'QUI FUIT MATHATHIAE', omitting the second 'QUI FUIT'. It is interesting to wonder whether it was contemplation of the beauty of this very genealogy, connecting as it does Christ to Adam, that inspired Archbishop Ussher to calculate the date of the Creation, and if so whether he spotted this error in time or not.

ui	fuit	machad
ui	fuit	iae
ui	fuit	semei
ui	fuit	ioseph osse
ui	fuit	iuda
ui	fuit	iohanna
ui	fuit	ressa
ui	fuit	zorbba
ui	fuit	salachiel
ui	fuit	hieri
ui	fuit	melchi
ui	fuit	addi
ui	fuit	cosan
ui	fuit	elmadam
ui	fuit	er
ui	fuit	iesu
ui	fuit	eliezer

PLATE XIX

THE GENEALOGY OF CHRIST
(Page 3)

Fol. 201R

By now the 'Q's are no longer letters; the birds have won the day and their attenuated bodies now form each 'Q'. Or do they? The 'Q's certainly have bird-like heads and legs, together with what appear to be vestigial wings, but the tails of the 'Q's seem to have changed into the hind quarters of animals, and a new line of snakes, birds and humans has appeared after the FUITs.

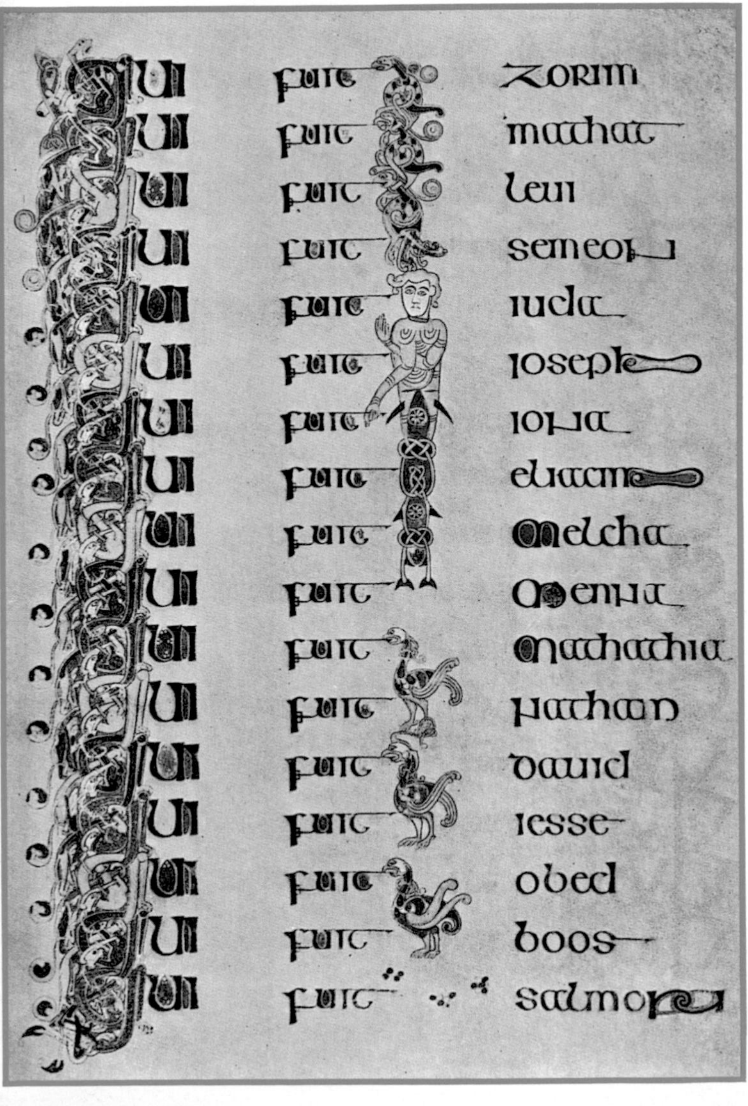

Qui fuit Zorim
Qui fuit matthat
Qui fuit leui
Qui fuit semeon
Qui fuit iuda
Qui fuit ioseph
Qui fuit iona
Qui fuit eliacim
Qui fuit Melcha
Qui fuit Menna
Qui fuit Mathathia
Qui fuit nathan
Qui fuit dauid
Qui fuit iesse
Qui fuit obed
Qui fuit boos
Qui fuit salmon

PLATE XX

THE TEMPTATION OF CHRIST

Fol. 202V

The passage represented here is the third and last temptation when the Devil said He could prove He was the Son of God by casting Himself off the roof of the Temple of Jerusalem. Christ is normally shown at this moment as a full-length figure, but other later manuscripts also depict him half-length, as here. The picture has a softness about it that distances it from other portraits in the manuscript and although it has been ascribed to the same artist as that of the Virgin (Plate II), Sullivan and others have suggested that the emaciated, black, tail-less devil is so out of character, and indeed proportion, with the remainder of the composition that it must have been added by a later, inferior hand. Carl Nordenfalk proposes that the profiled heads represent 'inhabitants of the monastery in which the book was made', but this misses the whole point of the temptation. What would be the purpose of floating miraculously down from the roof of the temple if the forecourt were not crowded with witnesses?

PLATE XXI

PORTRAIT OF ST JOHN

Fol. 291V

Though similar in its essentials to the Portrait of St Matthew (Plate V), and the 'Doubtful Portrait' (Plate VII), this picture differs from them in a number of details such as the heaviness of the frame, and the lack of the inner frame and arch. St John is much more definitely seated than either of his co-Evangelists, on a type of throne commonly to be seen in manuscripts from the Court School of Charlemagne. The enormous halo may have been given to the Evangelist by the artist to compensate for the informality of his posture. This portrait has suffered most from the book-binder's shears, but not as much as this particular reproduction would lead one to believe. In other reproductions the curtailed hand, which may be a later addition, beyond the left border is whole, and holds what appears to be a red nail, though Sullivan maintains it is a lighted taper.

PLATE XXII

THE OPENING WORDS OF
ST JOHN'S GOSPEL

Fol. 292R

The following words, 'IN PRINCIPIO ERAT VERBUM ET VERBUM', 'In the beginning was the Word, and the Word (was with God, and the Word was God.)' must be one of the most impressive openings to any piece of writing. Full justice is done to it here, in a plate strongly allied to that which introduces St Mark's Gospel and at the same time totally different from it. Here there can be no doubt that it is the Evangelist who appears, twice, at the head of the page, for in each case he holds a book. The monster, though, to whom he is so unconcernedly chatting in the right-hand picture seems to owe more to St Luke's Ox, albeit with a superfluity of horns, than to St John's own Eagle. Once again, it is the richness of ornament that captivates the eye, especially the combinations of circles at the four corners of the 'N', the delicate patterns on its uprights and the ingenuity of the crossbar.

PLATE XXIII

A PAGE OF INITIALS

From copies by Mrs Helen Campbell D'Olier

Fine as its set-pieces are, the chief joy of the *Book of Kells* are the illuminated initial letters which are scattered with generous abandon through every page of text. These letters distinguish the *Book of Kells* most from all other manuscripts in the Insular tradition. Though these are usually to be found on the left of the page, they are not always so. It is also far from uncommon to find even small letters in the middle of a line embellished with an extra twirl, or with their open areas filled with contrasting colours, or the inconvenient space at the end of a sentence filled with stars, or fish or birds. The examples on this page and the next are in fact taken from copies made with an accuracy and beauty unsurpassed even by the originals. On this page are shown three examples of black-letter initials (EXSURGENT, VESPER and BONUM) where the initial letter is written in ink and differs little from the rest of the text, except in size, and coloured adornment, and where subsequent letters diminish gradually in size until they merge gracefully into the rest of the text.

EXSURGENT

VESPER

OIIUM

PLATE XXIV

A PAGE OF INITIALS

From copies by Mrs Helen Campbell D'Olier

The 'P' of PROPTER and the letter 'R' in this plate are samples of the other great tradition of Celtic initial illuminating. In this, the basic form of the letter is retained, but drawn as a coloured ribbon with its extremities adorned with heads and limbs which bear no real relation to the letter but provide a harmonious extension of it. Note that the border of the ribbon is never a single line but is always embellished in some manner, usually as here by a fringe of red dots. Less commonly are the first 'I' of ET DIXIT in this plate and the 'P' of PO[nite] in Plate XXIII where the letter or part of it is actually formed by a recognizably complete animal forced into an unnatural posture by the demands of the letter. This is much more a continental tradition. Its use in an Insular manuscript such as the *Book of Kells* is another pointer towards the relative lateness of the work, just as the extensive use of mongrams, as in ET DIXIT, confirms its essentially Insular character. It is precisely this blending of so many distinct strands that gives the *Book of Kells* its unique charm.

ROPTER

BIBLIOGRAPHY

The principal sources used for this book have been:—

ALTON, E.H., MAYER, P. and SIMMS, G.O., *The Book of Kells* (3 vols). Facsimile edition with introduction and notes (Bonn, 1951)

BACKHOUSE, J., *The Illuminated Manuscript* (Oxford, 1979)

BACKHOUSE, J., *The Lindisfarne Gospels* (Oxford, 1981)

NORDENFALK, C., *Celtic and Anglo-Saxon Painting: Book Illumination in the British Isles 600—800* (London, 1977)

SULLIVAN, Sir E., *The Book of Kells* (London, 1920)

WESTWOOD, J. O., *The Art of Illuminated Manuscripts: Illustrated Sacred Writings* (London, 1988)

PICTURE ACKNOWLEDGEMENTS

INTRODUCTION
Carpet-cross from *Book of Lindisfarne*, British Library; Carpet-page from *Book of Durrow*, The Board of Trinity College Dublin; St Matthew from *Book of Lindisfarne* British Library.

PLATES
11, 15 and 20, The Board of Trinity College Dublin. All other images Studio Editions Ltd.